5th Grade ELA
Volume 1

© 2013
OnBoard Academics, Inc
Newburyport, MA 01950
800-596-3175
www.onboardacademics.com

ISBN: 978-1494860288

Table of Contents

Adjectives and Adverbs

Key Vocabulary

adjective

adverb

Adjectives and Adverbs

Find the adjective and adverb in this sentence and write them in the boxes provided.

| An adjective describes a noun or a pronoun, telling which one or what kind. | An adverb describes verbs, adjectives, or other adverbs, telling how, when, where, how often, or how much. |

 Tori played her old violin beautifully.

adjective	adverb

Adjective Adverb Summary

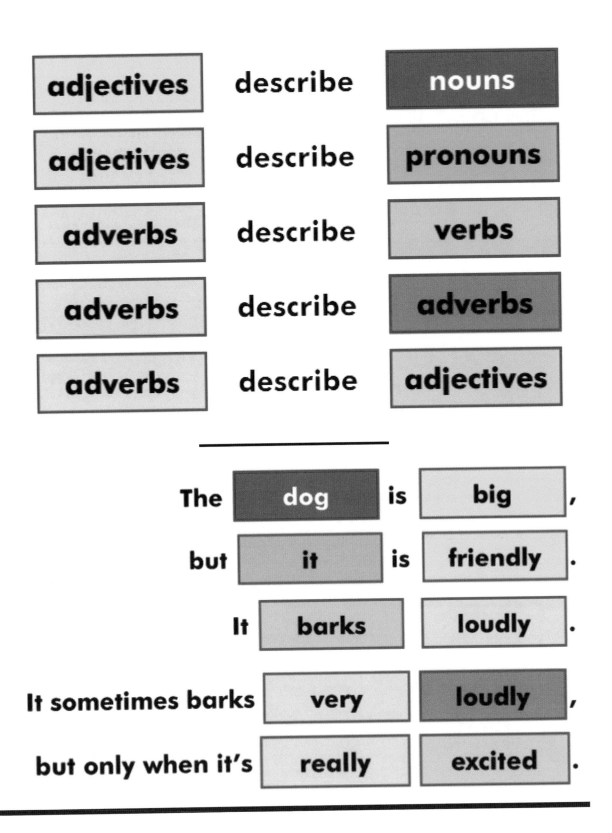

Label the word in red.

Mia looked **happy.**

Mia looked **up.**

| adverb | | adjective |

Sort the words using this Venn Diagram.

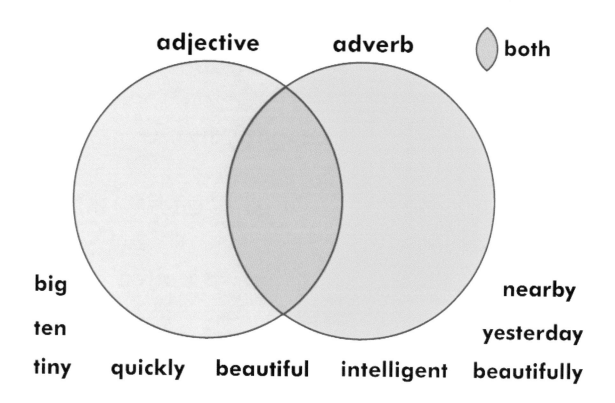

adjective   adverb   both

big

ten

tiny   quickly   beautiful   intelligent   beautifully

nearby

yesterday

Circle the how, when, where and how much adverbs.

Owen quickly tied his sneakers.

The big basketball game is today.

His teammates waited nearby.

They were very nervous.

Underline the adverbs in each sentence.

Yesterday, James was painting his room.

The telephone rang loudly.

James ran downstairs to answer it.

He accidentally spilled the paint.

He is always having accidents!

Classify the adverbs in terms of how, when, where and how often.

☐	Yesterday, James was painting his room.
☐	The telephone rang loudly.
☐	James ran downstairs to answer it.
☐	He accidentally spilled the paint.
☐	He is always having accidents!

how	how often	where	when

Name_____

Adjectives and Adverbs Quiz

1. Adjectives tell us where, when or how. True or false.

2. Identify the adjective: There are four students at each table.
   a. There
   b. four
   c. students
   d. each

3. Identify the adverb: The students worked silently unitl their work was complete.
   a. students
   b. worked
   c. silently
   d. complete

4. How is the word suddenly used in this sentence? Suddenly, I turned around.
   a. verb
   b. adverb
   c. adjective
   d. noun

5. Circle the adverb. The puppy ran playfully through the yard.

Parts of Speech Review

Key Vocabulary

noun

pronoun

verb

adjective

adverb

Nouns
Identify and classify the nouns.

person	place	thing

Mia took the bus to school.

The mouse scurried into its hole with the cheese.

David couldn't find his notebook and pencil.

Mr. Lee and Dr. Jones attended the conference.

Replace these nouns with pronouns.
Write the appropriate pronoun above the box.

| Fernando | likes to play the piano. | |

| Please pass me my socks; | the red socks. | |

| Tori and Alison | live in the same building. | |

| My mom and I | are going to see "Cats". | |

Verbs
Identify the verb in each sentence. Write the verb in the corresponding box.

1   Mia and Tori often study together in the evenings.

2   They often meet after dinner.

3   On Thursdays they have dinner together.

4   Mia likes Tori's off beat sense of humor.

5   She always laughs at her corny jokes.

1   _____

2   _____

3   _____

4   _____

5   _____

Adjectives
Fill in the blanks with adjectives.

The Mona Lisa is probably the most _____

 painting in the world. It took the artist,

Leonardo da Vinci, about _____ years to

complete, and depicts a woman sitting

upright with _____ arms and an

_____ smile. Vandalized on more

than _____ occasion, this _____ painting is

now safely displayed behind a _____

glass shield.

bullet-proof   iconic   enigmatic

famous   folded   16   one

_____

Which adjectives could replace the words enigmatic and iconic?
Write your answer above the word.

The Mona Lisa is probably the most famous painting in the world. It took the artist, Leonardo da Vinci, about 16 years to complete, and depicts a woman sitting upright with folded arms and an enigmatic smile. Vandalized on more than one occasion, this iconic painting is now safely displayed behind a bullet-proof glass shield.

Adjective or adverb?

Label the red word.

Mia looked happy.

Mia looked up.

| adverb | adjective |

Summary of adjectives and adverbs.

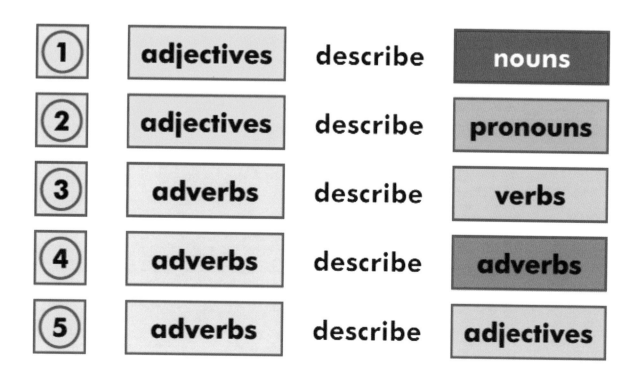

1	adjectives	describe	nouns
2	adjectives	describe	pronouns
3	adverbs	describe	verbs
4	adverbs	describe	adverbs
5	adverbs	describe	adjectives

Practice

Label the words taken out of this passage. The labels to be used are on the right side.

Last year, James entered the school's spelling bee competition. In the final round, he was asked to spell the word "onomatopoeia". He was very nervous, but he spelled it correctly and won the competition!

last ☐   final ☐   spelled ☐

James ☐   he ☐   correctly ☐

entered ☐   very ☐   won ☐

(N)oun
(P)ronoun
(A)djective
(V)erb
(adv) adverb

Name_____

Parts of Speech Review Quiz

1. He hurried down the street. The use of hurried is as a verb. True or false?

2. Alicia didn't want her cats in the bedroom.
   a. they
   b. those
   c. them
   d. she

3. What does the adverb silently describe? We finished our test silently so that the others in class could concentrate.
   a. the others
   b. finished
   c. our test
   d. concentrate

4. Circle the verb. We raced to the front of the long line.

5. Circle the adverb. The snail crept slowly across the walkway.

6. Circle the adjective. We raced to the front of the long line.

Conjunctions

Key Vocabulary

conjunction

coordinating conjunction

subordinating (subordinate) conjunction

compound sentence

independent clause

Conjunctions

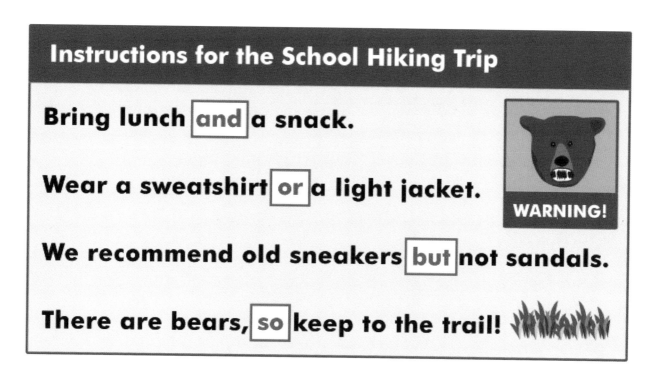

Instructions for the School Hiking Trip

Bring lunch and a snack.

Wear a sweatshirt or a light jacket.

We recommend old sneakers but not sandals.

There are bears, so keep to the trail!

WARNING!

Conjunctions link words, phrases, or clauses. The most commonly used conjunctions are and, but and or.

Conjunctions

Add conjunctions to this passage.

Hippos may look very friendly, [   ] they're not. Hippos [   ] Cape Buffalo are the two most dangerous large animals in all of Africa. Neither lions [   ] crocodiles cause as many human deaths. Hippos with young are especially dangerous, [   ] should be avoided at all times. Many people know about the dangers, [   ] still get too close to hippos and their young. Keep well back, [   ] you might regret it.

| nor | yet | and | so | or | but |

Coordinating Conjunctions

F	for
A	and
N	nor
B	but
O	or
Y	yet
S	so

Conjunctions are used as 'joiners', and coordinating conjunctions are used to join two equal parts together, e.g. Dad likes coffee and tea. The FANBOYS acronym may help you to remember the coordinating conjunctions.

Coordinating Conjunctions and Compound Sentences

Matteus is a good student. His penmanship is poor.

Coordinating conjunctions are used to join two equal parts together. When the equal parts are sentences, the new sentence is called a **compound sentence.** The two parts of the compound sentence are called **independent clauses.**

 Matteus

Matteus is a good student, but his penmanship is poor.

When a conjunction joins two independent clauses, it usually needs a comma.

Use coordinating conjunctions and rewrite the sentences as compound sentences.

Mia's Dad likes to play golf.
He is not very good at it.

Do you want pizza?
Would you rather have a sub?

Tori was bored.
She read a book.

Alison's mom is a teacher.
Owen's mom is an attorney.

Subordinating Conjunctions

The doctor examined the x-rays.
He concluded that Mia's leg was broken.

> Subordinating conjunctions **are used to connect** dependent clauses: **when one thing happens as a result of another.**

When the doctor examined the x-rays,
he concluded that Mia's leg was broken.

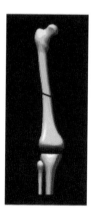

Commas

My allowance was increased because I made honor roll.

Because I made honor roll, my allowance was increased.

Fill in the blanks with subordinating conjunctions.

[_____] we put on our costumes, my sister and I went trick or treating. [_____] we got home, we counted up our treats. We had collected over 50 pieces of candy, [_____] some of it was out of date. I took off my mask, [_____] I wouldn't scare my baby brother. [_____] he is only 2, he doesn't really understand Halloween. [_____] we are new to the neighborhood, my parents wanted to inspect the candy. They said we shouldn't eat the cookies, [_____] we know the family. Sadly, some cookies had to go in the trash, [_____] they looked delicious!

even though	unless	so that	although
Since	Because	When	After

Name_____

Conjunctions Quiz

1. Because is a coordinating conjunction. True or false?

2. Which of these conjunctions is not a subordinating conjunction?
   a. although
   b. since
   c. or
   d. when

3. He did not complete his chores, _____ did he finish his homework.

4. I finished my homework on time, _____ I was able to play with my friends.

5. _____ my brother woke up late, we were late for school.
   a. After
   b. Unless
   c. Although
   d. Because

6. If a comma is needed, add it. Because I was full I skipped dessert.

Subject-Verb Agreement

Key Vocabulary

verb

pronoun

indefinite pronoun

Subject-Verb Agreement

> **What is the *subject* of the sentence? Is it singular or plural?**

Enter the correct verb.

My class [   ] taking a test on Monday.

is

are

> **Singular subjects have singular verbs; plural subjects have plural verbs. This is what is meant by the term subject-verb agreement.**

Add a verb to each sentence which 'agrees' in number with the subject of that sentence.

Owen and Mia ☐ patiently at the bus stop.

The school bus ☐ late.

School ☐ in ten minutes.

Their class ☐ a field trip today.

The children ☐ to head back.

Owen's or Mia's mom ☐ sure to be home.

waits	is	starts	has	decides	is
wait	are	start	have	decide	are

Pronouns also need subject-verb agreement.

Sanjeev is an excellent musician.

He plays piano and the flute.

Sanjeev is an excellent musician.

He plays piano and the flute.

Is or Are

Decide if the verb should be is or are and then enter it into the box.

The dogs and the cats [   ] responsible for the mess.

The dog and the cat [   ] responsible for the mess.

The dogs or the cat [   ] responsible for the mess.

The dog or the cats [   ] responsible for the mess.

When subjects are joined by and, they are always plural. When subjects are joined by or, the verb should agree with the subject closest to the verb.

The subject must agree with the verb.

> **Disregard phrases that modify or come between the subject and the verb.**

The car, one of several cars in the parking lot, looks old and in need of repair.

The car, one of several cars in the parking lot, looks old and in need of repair.

Choose the verb that agrees with the subject.

Choose the verb that agrees with the indefinite pronoun.

The committee, which consists mostly of lawyers, [____] meeting to discuss the proposal.

| is |
| are |

The principal, as well as most of the teachers, [____] against extending the summer vacation.

| was |
| were |

The old lady with all of the cats [____] there.

| lives |
| live |

An **indefinite pronoun** is a pronoun that refers to an unspecified thing or things. Indefinite pronouns include: *anybody, anyone, each, either, no one, both, others, several, all, most, none,* and *some.*

Eric and Kyle are half brothers.

Each [____] the same mother.

Both of them [____] a lot like her.

Everyone always [____] that.

Neither brother [____] their father.

Some of their DNA [____] totally different

and so some of their features [____] totally different too.

| has | looks | says | resembles | is |
| have | look | say | resemble | are |

Name_____

Subject-Verb Agreement Quiz

1. This sentence has subject-verb agreement: The group were the first to reach the summit. True or false?

2. Neither of the two pizzas _____ suitable for vegans.
   a. is
   b. are
   c. either A or B

3. Mr. Smith and Mr. Rocco _____ good candidates for the upcoming election.
   a. is
   b. are
   c. was
   d. were

4. Grandma, along with our cousins, _____ coming to the ceremony today.
   a. is
   b. are
   c. was
   d. were

5. The group of singers _____ nervous at first, but then relaxed as the perfromance went on.
   a. is
   b. are
   c. was
   d. were

Newburyport, MA 01950

1-800-596-3175

OnBoard Academics employs teachers to make lessons for teachers! We create and publish a wide range of aligned lessons in math, science and ELA for use on most EdTech devices including whiteboard, tablets, computers and pdfs for printing.

All of our lessons are aligned to the common core, the Next Generation Science Standards and all state standards.

If you like our products please visit our website for information on individual lessons, teachers licenses, building licenses, district licenses and subscriptions.

Thank you for using OnBoard Academic products.

Made in the USA
Lexington, KY
12 July 2015